AS THOUGH WE WERE FLYING

63 .

and.ᵧ

ᵗory arᵢ

org.uk

Andrew Greig is one of the leading Scottish writers of his generation. He has published eight collections of poetry, most of these with Bloodaxe, including *The Order of the Day* (Poetry Book Society Choice), *This Life, This Life: New & Selected Poems 1970-2006* and now *As Though We Were Flying* (2011). Known as 'the poet laureate of climbing', he publishes his collected poems of mountain adventures real and metaphorical as *Getting Higher* with Birlinn in 2011. Two books on his Himalayan expeditions have become classics in their field, as have *Preferred Lies* (a meditation on golf, self-recovery, Scotland) and *At the Loch of the Green Corrie* (fishing for Norman MacCaig, catching much else besides). His six novels include *That Summer* (Faber, 2000), *The Return of John Macnab* (Headline, 1996) and its late sequel *Romanno Bridge* (Quercus, 2008), and *In Another Light* (Weidenfeld & Nicolson, 2004), which was Saltire Scottish Book of the Year. He lives in Edinburgh and on Orkney with his wife, novelist Lesley Glaister.

ANDREW GREIG

As Though We Were Flying

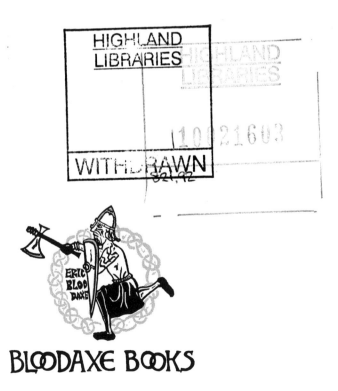

BLOODAXE BOOKS

ISBN: 978 1 85224 916 8

First published 2011 by
Bloodaxe Books Ltd,
Highgreen,
Tarset,
Northumberland NE48 1RP.

www.bloodaxebooks.com
For further information about Bloodaxe titles
please visit our website or write to
the above address for a catalogue.

Supported by
**ARTS COUNCIL
ENGLAND**

Cover design: Neil Astley & Pamela Robertson-Pearce.

Printed in Great Britain by
Bell & Bain Limited, Glasgow, Scotland.

To Dibby Greig and Imogen Isla French
a departure, an arrival

ACKNOWLEDGEMENTS

Acknowledgements are due to the editors of the following publications where some of these poems first appeared: *The Dark Horse, The Edinburgh Review* and *Scottish Review of Books*. 'A Long Shot' was published in the paperback edition of Andrew Greig's *Preferred Lies: A Journey to the Heart of Golf* (Phoenix, 2007).

CONTENTS

HOME FOR NOW

The Tidal Pools of Fife

I mind our town's tidal swimming pool –
changing huts, a sluice, rough concrete walls,
that fluid space folk clenched to enter.
Quick or slow, either way it really hurt
at first; shocked awake
by way of entertainment, as though pain
were the price of admission to the club,
as in a way it was, they shrieked and swam.
Thick-skinned and canny, those loons and quines
took pleasures won from work and hurt, knew
complete immersion in their lives, the release
of summer evenings, sprushed to the gills,
dancing on the Folly to the accordion.

All up our coast those outdoor pools
built by subscription between the Wars,
long pastel beaks of diving-boards
where folk dared or did not, the changing-huts
where couples dared or did not,
in time stopped holding water.
Too harsh, too raw – by the sixties
only we children went there, daring each other
with tales of congers in the slimy weeds,
vast lobsters lurking under slabs.
Now no one goes, no depth remains;
just broken walls, and slabs among the grass
like fallen tombstones, mark something happened here.

*

Old fishermen would gather at the harbour head
in a tilt of bonnets, mesh of cheekbones,
knots of arthritic hands, a swell of mufflers –
the moan and chuckle of old men
as their sons set out, doing well back then.

They thinned out, disappeared, were not replaced,
around the time the outdoor pools fell in.
I think of Alex Watson who never joined them
once he'd retired, disliking the sea,
though he had loved to swim
and dance on the Folly with his wife to be.
He sat uncomplaining as cancer ate him,
eyebrows like spray, quiet as haar.

He died in his Faith without fuss.
That man held no office,
made no fortune, only swam and danced,
worked and took the Scouts while children grew
(their graduation pictures crown Fife dressers,
embarrassed at the fuss but chuffed,
clutching the scroll that gets them out).
The kirk filled when he died, though he was
no one special, only one of them, so much so
he was their full and late expression,
like the outdoor pools they claimed for fun,
where people used to come for free
to laugh and share and swim,
filled to the brim with the gift of tides.

Raasay Revisited

The music of this world eludes us,
we agreed, crossing the building site,
yelling off-beat to the pile-driver.
In Inverarnish, we did not register
Pan-pipes in scaffolding when the wind backed east.

We walked to Clachan, where waves
broke without lament; among the pallid
stunted birch, we heard only white noise
and what was said between us
scarcely amounted to a lyric, even in Gaelic.

'The world has neither music nor meaning,'
said one of the more virulent among us.
'How we misrepresent these birds
when we say they sing.' None disagreed,
none felt better for his words.

Then Mairi stopped, raised one arm
like a tour guide, or someone at an auction
marking a new bid: *Cluinnidh mi e,*
I'm hearing them. Listen, m' eudail!
Her fervent vowels turned a dial

that let us tune to the atonal
Techno where her distant cousins nailed
corrugated roofing to the Albach Bar.
The sun went down behind Ben Cana
'And darkness came upon the kyles'

as we walked the ghostly woods of Hallaig,
hearing the dead and the unborn
through Sorley's 'straight and slender rowans'
croon waulking songs, *'Wet is the night,*
Come in my love.' Their pale arms beat

the densely-woven gloaming
to song-fabric that might cover us
through nights and sorrows we can't endure
unmantled. *Ceol bith-bhuan an t-saoghail.*
Still they don't understand us! Mairi called,

from the pierhead waved her hazel rod,
conducting through the mirk of our departure
music from bar and bard and woods;
we hear it still, far out beyond
the Sound of Raasay, MacLean's velvet drum.

Stronsay

The ferry left. A pause, then wake
slapping weed-furled timbers of the pier.
When that dispersed, sunlight hissed
through mussel beds. Clouds like toy ducks
sat on the horizon, the rest was blue all over.
On Shapinsay someone drove home a nail, then stopped.

We stared at each other.
Nothing but sound of the world turning
to throbbing on the inner ear:
annunciation, lady, matter announcing
over and over to itself it is with child.
I heard air drift over fine hairs on her wrist.

A boy stretched face-down on the pier,
jiggling a string into the depths.
Nothing moved anywhere save his hand and that string.
The world was so packed to the brim
any further motion was impossible. We were
sole witnesses to this

bored child on holiday – or source and centre
of the fullness, the silence flowing out from him,
lying as he was along the horizon, below duck-clouds,
while he stretched intent, peering down,
holding sea and sky and pier in place,
string rasping over wood, light feathering his hair.

Outlooks, Jimera de Libar

The rooster has wrecked his throat
now nights are no longer dark enough.
I think I know how he feels.

For weeks we might as well have been
in Scotland, beloved, but today
the hills across the valley quiver.

I write this from a damp chair on the terrace
while squadrons of swallows like tiny Spitfires
carve down out of the sun –

such massacres of the unseen thousands
when beauty feeds, and we reach
the limits of our sympathy!

Behind what hills does happiness hide
to lurk, brood, plot its return,
imperious as lengthening light?

We sit on, edgy with changed weather,
this new heat set against
the dreich and distant outlook of my home

which lingers like a throb of rheumatism
beneath our browning skins
as on a blameless afternoon

we sit on the terrace with *dos cervezas*
watching a train of empty cloud-carriages
shunt down the valley,

while the fruit we can so nearly
lean over the balcony to pick
are so nearly ripe.

Peterboro, Ontario

What lives now is winter, that day
I borrowed Kevin's skis to cross-country

the old trails, past shuttered cabins,
through woods, onto the frozen lake.

White beyond whiteness, void
indefinitely extended – I slid out

for island and the shore beyond, not sure
if it would hold, nor how much I cared

till half-way out, ice caved in behind.
Head-up, all-out, legs thrashed

fast as arms could pump, freed
of any other option, any need but

that far shore, yelling forgotten songs,
cursing and defiant, the heart engorged.

Then I was skimming over fear,
ice holding, snow parting, lips split in wonder –

dizzy joyous race, moving alone
over flat white space, knowing

how much one wants to live, yet may not!
Uncoordinate, out of time, compact with onrush,

I crashed into the shore,
lay gasping *I'm no awa tae bide awa!*

I'm no awa tae leave ye! Cracks boomed
across the ice, the lake settled down.

*

I sit in bed on a dreich Scots dawn,
drinking tea in my late middle years, feeling myself

sliding further out, more fearful, more bedazzled.
Day spreads on the duvet like a gasp

as though memory were a frozen loch
bearing us up where we can never

be again, committed, ecstatic, surrendered
to whatever comes next – and later

heading through trees at dusk, past pioneer fences,
distant barking, lights through pines,

towards the place that is not home but must be
home for now, as the body is, gliding through

a world traversed with stabbing poles,
twin planks of polished wood.

In Endcliffe Park

A speck of dust no weightier than a thought
must have touched dead water.
I did not see what started it, but watch the ring
expand as though the pool is shaping *O!*
while I stand with the same exclamation
widening through me.

Could the Porter Brook, this autumn park,
the fallen and the falling leaves,
this calm pool and the weir beyond, the onrush
to Stinky Bob steaming on his bench in the sun,
all the snags and graces with which things go downhill,
be best regarded not as material
but one long, complex thought of autumn
on this sector of the planet in its circuit round the sun,
one beat in that catchy theme
The Way Things Are?

And, more usefully, as I watch that circle spread
and these words begin enlarging on a momentary calm,
might we consider what arises in our minds
as nothing other than water, sky, trees, seasons,
and we who see ourselves as moving through the world
are better seen as receptacles, hosts
of the becoming that moves through us,
the pool in which its dust is registered and spread?

FIVE FIFE POEMS

In Sillar Dyke

The fishermen's stores were founded on tide-wrack
and the ancient harbour wall,
                            wave-breaker,

dull and undulating, is little more
than the sand it will be again.
Only thrawnness holds it there.

A retired fisherman wakes early in Cellardyke,
gropes downstairs, feeling himself kept company
by his habits, the specific ache

in his knees, and an isolation
so faithful one is never alone.
God knows he never liked the sea.

It was a job, no more.
In the ordered half-light of the kitchen
he watches fog inside the windows

fade away; in this unforeseen hour
the presences that have breathed here all night
are taking their leave,

old crew-mates who will soon receive him,
hoist high in the dripping
purse net of their arms.

Eck Hutchinson

The family house is sold,
I don't go back much any more.
The one who comes to mind tonight
I scarcely knew: Eck Hutchinson
set out for lobster off Fifeness
on a rowdy day, trusting his youth, his eye, his luck,
wanting *a pocket o siller* for the waddin.
A week later he washed up
eyeless, luckless, ageless.

She married later, her children have left home;
Eck Hutchinson remains
snagged at nineteen on those skerries,
however many waves break over them, and us.

A Life Change

(by the Dreel burn)

Grant we might take advantage and live
among back-country hawthorn,
shape-changed; perched on a branch
be an unexpected addition
to the tree of the living sentence,
head raised to leaf-broken sky.

Kaiplie Caves

I would walk again on Ne'er Day
the low coast to Kaiplie, where wet fields
gleam under wind, that barber's strop
putting an edge on Eternity,
and come at last to caves adopted
by monks, the dispossessed, then smugglers,

then nothing but the odd damp teenager.
He thinks of Vimto and the fisherman's daughter
as he crawls into the deepest cave
below what he thinks a fancy-free land,
to emerge into a glowing chamber
where sixty-six candles burn on ledges.

Observance without witness, silence without hearer,
was this ritual abandoned, or as it were
set in motion and *left running*,
as he did? There's aye something
never quite accounted for – a glint of moisture
in the eye of a lover who never really liked you,

those Ne'er Day flames in that dour place –
that make them linger still, like young Eck,
or Alex Watson, fisherman who never liked the sea.
Whoever you are now homes in
past darkening skerries, towards last light
bleeding down on Sillar Dyke.

Roost

And after all, what is it *for*,
the way a certain place comes home

to roost, at failing light,
within your branching ribs?

Wings spread, then fold;
claws ratchet, eyes close.

Nothing stirs
but that raptor which cries

only when it's hunting.
You jolt awake –

claws stir, eyes open,
the wings of Fife spread wide.

The Edinburgh Coliseum

I didn't know Romans had got this far.
How could I live so long in Edinburgh
among basalt plinths, these crumbling
red sandstone walls, and somehow failed
to grasp their ethos? Among the last
desultory tourists I walk, read, click, drift.
It's not so much the site itself bewilders
(Rome, after all, had one first and bigger)
but that I'd missed it, that disturbs me.

Yet it's all here: walls, tunnels, underground streets,
the secret alley where failed leaders could
be hurried away when the show turned bad;
the prisons, Zoo, the extensive training grounds,
the church where the fighters would be blessed.
Here is the balcony for the high ones, here
the proconsul's box (it seems the emperor
seldom showed up this far North,
preferring to rule from his southern comforts –
the show had its uses, but left him bored).
We can sit on the bum-smoothed stone
where the people lounged, gulped beer and oysters,
gawped, yelled, gambled, and cursed
their favourites going down, all engrossed
at others' triumphs, losses, deaths
while hip commentators carved on this old wall
thoughts on 'the society of the spectacle'.
The last cheers die, the fires dim,
through these same streets the crowd stream
sated or aroused, yet queasy and unsure
whether they've seen too little or too much.

Information boards are useful, but make me yawn.
So many animals killed! So many swans!
Audiences couldn't get enough swan fighting swan
till tastes hardened to swan-on-human action.

So much cheering, blood, re-enactment of great battles
amid this crucible of army, church, rulers, the people!
And I wake thinking *Yes of course*
Rome ruled here – look round at the crags,
the castle, Lawnmarket, the ruinous schemes; consider
our past eight hundred years. As footpads, dossers
and night patrols scuffle behind the museum,
and the consul's carriage glides by the Coliseum
while drunks screw in the dried-up fountain
in the moon-drenched Princes Street Gardens,
you can see clearly how it was. And is.

Park Mill

If a boy stands in Long Field and yells,
keeps silent as his cry goes out
over head-high barley to Park Mill,
in time a call comes back   *Hello hello!*
It doesn't sound entirely his own.
So he has to shout again in case
there really is someone across the way
who happened to start calling the same moment.
Are you there? Are you still there?

If the day is very still and he waits on,
from the wall of his home behind him
the call ricochets again   *hello   hello*,
and he imagines more than hears someone gasp
in fragments from Park Mill   *The re   the re*
and for the first time glimpses
what you start when you open your mouth.

I stand in Long Field in my father's coat.
He's long gone, sheep graze over Park Mill,
from neck down not a cell of me is the same.
I check no one's watching, throw arms wide and call.
Wait   and wait some more
till a cry comes back across the burn,
Hello hello   that voice not entirely my own.

I feel my bones as never before,
turn up the collar of my father's coat and shiver.
The wind mutters I am not the caller but the echo,
and it was my estranged voice that boy heard
cry across the distance, fifty years ago,
Are you there? Are you   still   there?

Wynd

It's back again, the how of rain
pleating off leaky roans, binding
strands that curve down stanks, curl
by high-walled wynds and dreels,
past sweetie shops with one faint bulb,
bell faltering as the pinnied widow
shuffles through from her back room –
What can I do you for the day?
She hands me now
no Galaxy or Bounty Bar
but a kindly, weary face, smear
of lipstick for her public, the groove
tartan slippers wore in linoleum
from sitting-room to counter, over thirty years:
the lost fact of her existence.

Currents ravel past the draper's
where Mr Duncan and his unspeaking sister
sort shirts by collar size, set out
Mason's cuff links and next season's vests;
on stiff white cards their flowing pens
price elastic, Brylcreem, dark tartan braces.

Floods tangle, splice, uncoil
down Rodger Street, past bank and tearoom,
the dodgy garage where they sold airguns to anyone,
the steamed-up window of the 'Royal'
where fires warms the bums of men who like
to drink standing, bunnets jammed down tight.
At Shore Street the rain-river
leaps the pavement, scours a channel
through pongy weed behind the sea wall
where damp frocks shiver under umbrellas
by the market cross, waiting for their lucky day
or at least the bus to Leven –
which won't come for ages, because it's Sunday.

In the hours between *Stingray* and the evening meal,
when the strings of family, place and history
working us, are all too bleeding visible,
as gutters burst the adolescent wonders
whether to have a quick one or read French poetry.
Smouldering with solitude, the prince of boredom
stands at the window, watching rain,
wondering when life ends, or will finally begin.

Fall, flow and ache.
By those cramped streets, the kenned wynds,
loans, closes, byways, dreels,
the dying shops, fishermen's damp houses
with empty sail lofts, broken pantiles,
wash-houses not ready for witty conversion;
by the constricting, cherished dreichness of our town
whose high tide had ebbed before ours began;
by the draper with its yellow blinds pulled down,
the angle of a bent streetlamp,
the budgie cage in old Jeanie's window;
by the secret path behind the allotment,
the steep slalom of Burial Brae,
the short-cuts, the dank kirks and graveyards –
by these details we did not know we loved,
we grew up provincial, in the heart of the world.

You are standing at the bedroom window
watching rain, homework abandoned on the desk.
The parents are somewhere unimportant,
wee brother plays keepie-uppie in the gloom –
time to belt the shorty raincoat, go
in search of nothing but the life to come.

Holly

Askew lane walked in drizzle
to Cuban boot heels echoing,
solitude marking its beat.

Sycamores drip black lopped limbs
where long-dead whalers' houses
shrug gable-ends at the sea.
In her swimsuit Stella smiles invitingly
from last night's lager can,
stoved in, out of date.
You back-heel her down a grate.
Whatever you are after, it's not that.

At the wynd-head someone leans,
unbolting an outhouse door.
She's been sent to put away her father's car,
a class-mate you'd sparked with at her party
though nothing more, you being blate
and this East Fife, where the ancient cult
of virginity for clever girls, early pregnancy
for the rest, had two years left to run.
In those days you knew little more
than differential calculus and irregular verbs,
but you knew what came next would be
definitive as Sunday in the shrouded town.
Salt in the rain on her full mouth.

*

Holly wore jeans with a man's front fly
before any lass in Fife.
She kept stapled copies of *Spare Rib*
below a mattress in the old sail loft.
When she'd proffered them it was
far cry from girls on lager cans
with 'Buy me' in their eyes.
I'd thought patriarchy meant the Russian Church
but through the static of rage and wit
I got the message that at last
not everything was down to me.
Sweet Mary, the relief!
Piled fertiliser bags against the door,
old sacks on the mezzanine floor,
in the petrol-smelling dark we got by on feel.

Wobbly-kneed, late for tea,
at the wynd-head I turned up
my shorty raincoat collar –
not cool but blown, thoughtless, free.
Soft in the hips, seeing everywhere
eyes dark blue as mussel shells,
all night there lingered
over the white noise of the sea,
a cry without words, her on my astounded fingers.

THE LIGHT OF DAY

The best thing a dream

The best thing a dream can do for you
is not prophecy
nor free entertainment from your inner lunatic

not even the message
your mind is holed below the waterline
and will sink fast unless
you can find that length of rope
you let slip overboard last year

(it's good to know the secret sharer of your life
a calm and I think magnificently bearded second-mate
– your first mate, beardless, sleeps beside you –
remains on watch throughout the night)

No the best thing a dream
can do is remind you
it's not true

and the distressed lady
bearing her mutilated liver in a handbag
will not die
not because you've saved her or failed her
as you rummaged frantically through her entrails
but because she does not exist

It's worth being reminded your mind
does this kind of thing most often
when you're wide awake
(especially the distressed ladies)

and to truly wake up is to know the reason
you cannot grasp that rope underwater
is there is no rope nor water
only grasping

Oh to surface beside an entire lover
and feel your fingers slowly unhook
one by painful one!

First light, Edinburgh

Propped in bed watching
dawn decant on the city,
I look at the book then back at the sky.

Though the book does not claim to be
the word of God,
I do not defend myself when it speaks to me.
Though this tea is brown and tannin-dry
it clears the windows of the eyes
as though they really open on a soul.
Though this oatcake contains no sugar
it bears honey to my lips.
Though the woman singing in the kitchen is but five foot one
and breakfast is solo foraging in this house,
she contains all that is dear and she feeds me.

*

May the sky like a gleaming ewer
daily tip and pour its liquor in.
May the plug of the heart pop open,
let it all flow back out again.

Now sky, book, tea, oatcake
refloat this city's battered hulk
as though it were seaworthy,
as though we had some place to go,

our sails filling with the least
puff of the world.

A Long Shot

As your lover on waking recounts her dreams,
unruly, striking, unfathomable as herself,
your attention wanders
to her moving lips, throat, those slim shoulders
draped in a shawl of light, and what's being christened here
is not what is said but who is saying it,
the overwhelming fact
she lives and breathes beside you another day.

Other folks' golf shots being even less interesting
than their dreams, I'll be brief.
While she spoke I thought of a putt yesterday at the 4th,
as many feet from the pin as I am years from my birth,
many more than I am from my death:
one stiff clip, it birled across the green,
curved up the rise, swung down the dip
like a miniature planet heading home,

and the strangest thing is not what's going to happen
but your dazed, incredulous knowing it will,
long before the ball reaches the cup then drops –
that it's turned out right after all,
like waking one morning to find yourself
unerringly in love with your wife.

Button

Without looking,
they find each other's hand.

She fits below his oxter,
he fits into her mind.

In the morning, putting on a shirt,
we push button through eyelet

without checking,
thinking of something else,

doing it right
by feel alone.

A Swing of the Axe

'Sometimes an axe was placed in the crops with the cutting edge to the skies'

Days like sodden logs line up in the rain.
Here's to the few times we go
with the grain of our own life

and know it
as wood knows the cutting edge
when it splits wide open.

The Church of Today

'The church of today...'
The phrase detached
from the radio, hovered,
took shape above
the tea and toast.

She is gaping in the kitchen nave;
hands folded on the formica
altar of the breakfast table,
she admires the diffraction
rose window in a smeary pane.

Outside, small birds
sermonise on mating, territory,
the need to eat.
She greets them, they leave:
her favourite kind of preacher.

The humble church of today,
let us attend it faithfully,
light candles in our minds
so we may brave even the crypt
opening in the chest at night.

Nine Steps to the Shed

Out the back door,
mug in one hand, biscuit in the other,
to step on the first of nine
off-round uneven sandstone slabs
the size and shape of mammoth's footprints
that stomp across the soggy grass
dividing house from shed,
and feel yourself following in the bulk
of something patient, vast, fissured –
Deep Past, say, or a world yet undeclared –
on this transit from one space to another.

What's down there today? Yellow-white splatter
from a passing gull, last week's nosebleed,
the snail lurched sideways in its crunched house,
a phrase that descended earlier
on your bowed head in the shower –
enough to be going on with.

These stones are split
from the bed of Lake Orcadie
which swelled and shrank over these parts –
fresh water, ocean, dried up, fresh again, salt,
this happened many times – and stony shades
of shellfish and minnow now lurk between
flouts of fronds and weeds, squashed
with utter delicacy and absolute power
by the weight of ages passing overhead
(crunch of that snail in the dark last night),
in the way stray memories from the vanished
lake of a life endure, distorted, flattened,
set in stone as we pause on the way
to the place of reckoning.

So small a space to contain
imagined pachyderm, the fossils and the lake,

the trail of stones that lead you
to pause with one hand on the door!
Glance at the world you're passing through,
small fry with Time pressing on your neck
even as you bent under the shower's benediction,
look back at the nine stones, this staggered line
between one dwelling and the next,
then step into the different light.

The Natural Order: blackbird

It's spring, and one fat blackbird whistles on the ledge
and from the shed our albino blackbird
whistles whitely back – or did she start it,
he merely echoed her desire?
Who knows. I seldom wake that early.

Call and response, response and call,
who can pronounce upon
the order of it all?
But we who always assumed the world
took our cue, may come to suspect
we speak back the world after a brief delay

and the length of that lapse
is exactly the distance we stand
without the garden we are standing in.

The Luncheon of François Aussemain and Erzébet Szántó

His Paris? Her Budapest?
This rendezvous of bulging intellects
must be neutral ground – thus Edinburgh.

The logos of Georgian: harmony so unshakeable,
no clues what gives within, she thinks,
zipping up her flight bag. Suits me, pal.
And Aussemain? Remembering how icy Occam's
Razor cut-throated through High Street closes,
he packs a vest beneath his shirts: canny man.

Szántó strides Princes Street Gardens in Doc Martens.
Her dark green three-piece tweed suit has left
its maker no spare cloth whatever: how very Erzébet!
Here comes Aussemain in pale linen – apparently Hegel's
blue velvet smoking-jacket is mere scurrilous rumour.
Just as well – even ironically, it would be unforgivable.

The scent of him still forty metres off – the engine
oil of that whirring brain, she registers,
has the odour of petunias, slightly gone.
Approaching, she claps a hand to her eye, fiddles.
Surely to God she is not wearing a monocle!
No, just a troublesome lens. An opening there.

In the sunlit café below the Castle they bat about
the true nature of *grit*   in resolve, the soul, the eye.
It's bound for the Forth, dear colleague. Here's my hanky.
I think not, she replies. *Thank you.*
Having this far descended from noble strata,
This grit is bound for nada, some cry it nirvana.

He examines the menu and (covertly) her eyes.
That heart's knot will never be untied.
Nevertheless, he reflects, this too is constancy.
The choosing of a starter, like one's first spouse,
being pressurised by hunger, is invariably flawed,
F.A. observes. *Mistaken, yet not entirely regretted.*

She considers his pale face over dazzling zinc.
The waiter hovers, never quite lands.
Wise to have low expectations, friend,
of the entrée; the middle years leave one feeling full
without quite remembering why. Personally,
I pass on them wherever possible.

Then again, dear colleague, he taps perfect fingernails
on his milky Pernod glass (her hands
bitten to the quick, sturdy, deft as her lips) *all desserts*
– Are just! they chorus. Then she adds
The karmic pudding: late sweetness if you're good?
Their eyes greet: conker-brown, witch-hazel. Do not avert.

In all the years of correspondence through essay,
monograph, review, the question of his sexualité
has not been raised. And she is as she is,
buttoned in immaculate tight tweed.
A pause. He orders cognac. She passes
but raises his glass to her lips, sips,

rotates the glass. He looks at it, at her crowded, brilliant face
in Northern sunlight: no equivocation here.
His eyes on hers, he drinks where her lips have been.
The bill awaits, but the only chestnut raked from the fire
of Western Thought still left unshelled
is that pre-Socratic chestnut: his hotel, or hers?

Hang on! You suggest that metaphysical flâneur
and the severe task-mistress of the minotaur
roaming the socio-political-cultural labyrinth of Europa –
both so freely quoted by the fashionable (ça existe?)
poets of our day, to bring some gravity to the least
weighty of their verses – *got it on in Edina?*

Point taken. They would never have agreed which hotel.
But lately Aussemain pins a tiny ruby grouse on his lapel,
and at our interview Szántó's hands stray over
a glowing chestnut that, she admits, once fell
from those trees that rise above the Almond river
in its most private upper waters.

The Natural Order: thrush

Such an old thing new,
pine needles sprung
sharp on fading sky
as missal thrush hits topmost twig,
clings on, sings –

What passes here
when an outer shift is echoed by one inside,
and we realise all the time
we've had it the wrong way round?
The dummy we thought inert
speaks first
and we find our lips repeat
What we thought ours is theirs
What we thought theirs is ours.

The bird opens its tiny mouthpiece
and after the slightest lapse
I croak
We are the bird at the top of the tree
through which it sings
its needly heart out.

An Edinburgh Encounter

A young woman walks
our chill sunny street
alone, confiding to the air
I am off to the shops.
I'll make somethin nice for tea –
we'll hae a bath thegether!

When I was her age,
I'd have known she was a nutter,
talking to nothing like it cared.
Does our inner life not grow
best like a mushroom in moist dark,
silently, alone? Silly woman.

Old grump. When we pass,
she is not talking to a phone,
the brown sack across her chest
is not shopping.
– It's such a bonnie morn
we'll go the long way, darlin –

The flicker of white in her sling
is not a mobile phone
but a new baby slung
in its mobile home.

Silly old grump
leading himself up the garden path,
opens the door and goes inside
cradling that encounter to his chest.

Love beyond reason glimpsed in the street.

Married Lovemaking

When they made love, those afternoons
in the purple squat, the tenement room,
the pine-clad flat, the house with mad wallpaper,

their opening was practised, as a croupier
lays out and retrieves the deck in one
fluttering sweep, then lets the game begin.

Stay with that sense of skilful ease
but change the line of imagery to this:
when bellies touched

then softened, there seemed few ways
to go, to just one goal,
but always something new struck home –

how dark that lowered lash, how slim
her wrists today, the crease doubling
the edge of his mouth as he smiled –

then the thousandth time became *this time*,
and gates they had not known
closed till then, swung open:

they are where they've never been before,
domains there are no words or maps for,
no paths at all but those

cleared by each caress, as though
one finger re-directs the stream,
a murmur elevates those trees.

His response lays harebells underneath,
her eyes propels the bird
downstream to blue the air;

where branches part above the river ,
they jump together, plumes
rising like wings as they plunge.

In time they surfaced, opened eyes to see
the ceiling back again, the old friend breathe.
Wanting nothing more but more of this,

the place that they must leave,
they would lie a while, drifting,
her world-defining hand uncurled on his.

A Simple Evening

It was a simple evening –
rare enough round these parts
where great knots form as by themselves,
binding word and thought and memory
till one can scarcely move or breathe.

The start of a line snagged
in the angle formed by a magpie's neck
against the falling light in the square outside
where the municipal fountain rose and fell,
and led to my father's baize table
where he'd sit alone and deal four bridge hands
beneath this very standard lamp.
Asked how he could bid against himself, he said
The trick is to act as though
you don't know what you do know.

It must have been the old man let me hook
a pencil round the other loose end of the line
and steady movement across an A4 page unwound
length after length of that false knot as though
the universe or my intestinal tract were coming undone,
till something was left as simple and direct
as a piece of string the length of
a piece of string.

Seen from above
a man of a certain age is resting in an armchair
beside a standard lamp by a green baize table
where lies an A4 sheet on which someone has written
It was a simple evening
rare enough round these parts...

As the magpie folds its wings for the night
the man is wondering what kind of poem includes itself
and how, if ever, it could end –
yet what kind of life does not bear itself
as both content and witness to its own passing,
as though a fountain endlessly threw up
the water that lies still and reflects itself
tossing the same water
into the failing light above the public square?

From a Marriage Bed

It is late, no doubt. Muscles of the eye
give out, pages blur. In any case
your mind's elsewhere. The beloved,
met late in life, is late returning!
The moon has skewed the Velux to
this parallelogram of light that frames
her nightdress in the corner where
she stood by the mirror this morning,
surveyed herself with that assessing
unfooled eye that looks on you each day...

You have abandonment issues, no doubt.
Blind not to, at this late hour.
The beloved with whom you've sworn
your ashes will be mixed and flung
on winds that rake the Bay of Skaill
may be drinking the strong wine
of women's friendship, or walking home
past trees and benches furred with hoar,
thinking she is next to nothing
as the joyrider's car mounts the kerb...

The street door clicks, clunks to.
Light switch, keys on table, shoes drop.
Sink tap groans, she hums the last
song from where she's come.
Now she'll be lifting the green towel...

One moon on all the chimney pots'
sleeping or extinguished fires, this
beating chest, her step up the stair:
two people, two lives, one house,
it is very strange.

A MOMENT'S LIBERTY

A Light in the North

(i.m. Gunnie Moberg)

Towards the end she moved outside
to lie and watch mind's weather
re-shape as clouds

now bull   now bear   but mostly
like nothing much at all
nearly always like nothing much at all

just her witnessing circumstance
sensing how coming and going
brewing at the heart of it

is all that keeps it up there
Cloud after all is heavier than air
always falling while re-building above

so it looks like it is hovering
as might someone without a parachute
seem perfectly sustainable

as long as the Earth keeps on
falling away beneath her
and as fast as cells are dying

new ones are being born
It is almost as though
she is not falling at all

but for the tears raised by her velocity
the way her clothes billow
and the sense that she is closing

on the witness below
calmly watching herself fall
as though she were 'flying'

as though she were flying

A Shetland Shawl

So many years, so full of holes.
What's left tonight
is off-white, brown and sepia,
like the Shetland shawl you bought her
somewhere, sometime...

– Mostly nothing at all
yet warm about the shoulders
through a long night in an Orkney chair
as you sit with a half bottle
in the drawer behind your shins,

drawing the length of a life
through the hole of a wedding-ring.

From the Royal College of Surgeons of Edinburgh

My only talent lay in these.
My father rubbed his hands together,
stared as though their whorls encoded
thirty years obstetric surgery.
It's manual craft – the rest's just memory
and application. The chief art
lies in knowing when to stop.

He curled his fingers, a safe-cracker
recalling a demanding lock;
I glimpse a thousand silent break-ins;
the scalpel's shining jemmy pops
a window in the body, then – quick! –
working in the dark remove or
re-arrange, then clean up, quit,
seal the entrance. Oh strange burglar
who leaves things better than he found them!
On good days it seemed my fingertips
could see through skin, and once inside
had little lamps attached, that showed
exactly how and where to go.
He felt most kin to sparks and joiners,
men whose hands would speak for them.

I wander through the college, meet
portraits of those names he'd list,
Simpson, Lister, Wade and Bell,
the icons of his craft, recalled
as though he'd known them personally.
Impossible, of course. Fingers don't see.
Yet it gave me confidence, so I could proceed.

I stare at the college coat of arms,
that eye wide-open in the palm,
hear his long-dead voice, see again
those skilful hands that now are ash.

Working these words I feel him by me,
lighting up the branching pathways.
Impossible, of course, yet it gives
me confidence – we need
belief we are not working blind;
with his eye open in my mind
I open the notebook and proceed.

Pin Head

But what can we say of what opens up when we close our eyes?
How measureless a world the blind must inhabit! I reel, astounded...
FRANCOIS AUSSEMAIN, Autres Pensées

Close your eyes.
What remains is practically
the shape and size
of the head of a pin.

Gleaming, round, smooth, it resembles nothing
so much as a highly charged dance floor
for atoms done up to the nines
where you chassis ecstatically (as you seldom did in life)
with your beloved in your arms.
You turn with your mother in your arms.
You are spinning with your father in your arms.
Every love you've ever known, however brief or shaming,
grandparents, teachers, friends, even the odd family dog
is clasped in your arms as you take a turn round the floor
to Quickstep, Shimmy, Hippy Hippy Shake,
while the band marks time over
the ragged be-bop of your pulse.

All this turns
on something the size of the head of a pin
that is stuck
alongside a myriad of others
in the plush pincushion of interstellar space
which is kept in a corner of the sewing box
of something so vast and forgetful
it seldom remembers to sew –

like your mother who sits all morning
looking out the window at the passing show,
a few buttons short
on the cardigan she has had so long

she has no idea where it came from,
or when she last looked inside
that sewing box in the corner.

She remembers this much: in the War,
people died, and they all loved to dance,
and lived when they could, from the heart.

A Girl I Knew

A girl I knew in South Alberta
pulled off her clothes and ran
the rough planks of the jetty,
flexed then shot her own
pale arrow into blue.

Thirty years later
she surfaces, streaming water and laughter,
stands on the far bank,
self-mocking, unreachable, triumphant.
She waves once, then dives away.

Our friends the dead are swimming from us now.
Their disappearance I can understand;
the reappearing act,
I don't know how they do that,
nor how much more often I can applaud.

Late Style

We are refined to this:
my hand on your arm as we watch TV,
your lips wordless on my chest in sleep.

May we live long enough
to come to the end of saying
and begin again
on the slopes of Ben Wyvis
when I turned to say
My heart is beating fast
I so need to kiss you

and you will startle then open
arms, heart and lips to me
as I open mine to you today:
beloved, you are the one decision
I have not second-guessed,
wanting only more and more
of this, and this, and this.

This Pilgrimage

You thought you really thought that being smart,
canny, clear-sighted and unfooled,
you would avoid all mess and lasting hurt.
You believed you really did believe
that having no beliefs you would not
fall for any daft ideas,
as though being non-judgemental would save you
having to be anyone at all. *Sweet Jesus!*

You're the one who spent two years
with your first lover deciding whether to marry
(you made lists *for* and *against*!)
and then did. Only someone with a degree
in Mental Philosophy could be that stupid.

I think that was when you gave up thinking
being clever was much use, and turned instead
to study your own heart,
about which you apparently knew nothing.
There followed a messy period.

And it hurt it really hurt, and there was nothing
to be done about it, and that was something
new to you, and you began to realise
other people are not stupid, careless or alien
when they too make a mess of their life.
Still you felt you really felt that being open
to every lover about the state of your heart
(which resembled nothing so much as a bomb attack
in rush-hour, when panic tramples manners
on the rush for Exits) was really playing fair.

It wasn't entirely your fault when you had friends
who believed who really believed having the correct
political analysis of the world you live in

actually justifies not handing spare change
to a shivering soul on her cardboard mat,
As your mother would say in her indiscreet old age:
Well fuck that.

For twenty years you followed *thought*, and for the next
twenty you followed *feeling*, and still you wander
lost in the back lanes of this world
as though you're not really from these parts.
My dog knows her way home better.

It's a miracle you have a Beloved
you will love and work with to the end,
She has her pilgrimage, you have yours.

    *

What did you *not* get wrong?
A hand on a coral nightgown through a winter night,
that was not heartlessly laid on.
Lying on a bench in a service station,
looking up twenty thousand feet into blue sky and clouds
feeling your soul abruptly explode from your chest
like an airbag from the steering column,
that was no accident.

When you held your father's hand before he died and was scared,
tentatively at first and then very tight,
that was a good grip.

Days spent in your country's hills
from Blà Bheinn to Conival,
in sun and wind and sleet and snow:
ice and judgement, joy and mortal terror,
then staggering home roped up with Mal
through dusk towards lit windows, beer and laughter,
those days were worth waking for.

And love, sex, tenderness, all that met
and failed to meet when bodies merged and flurried
in Canada and Queensferry, the cellar or your granny's bed,
the back of a Beetle in the Pentland hills,
in the sea at Goa, on the Brough of Deerness, very slowly
at nineteen thousand feet up the Baltoro,
so many beds, tears, raptures, rueful laughter –
however confused, mistaken or amoral
something human happened there.

The markers you took time to make
along the way, won't halt anything, you knew that.
Yet you kept on making them,
not from ambition but for their own sake.
That was not work nor paper wasted.

Those mornings you sat in the meditation huts
near Big Buddha, on Ko Samui,
the sea beneath, the golden wheel set on the rocks:
that was not tourism.

One thing does not change:
it is still possible for me to look down
on you, my striving journeyman,
and see you on some kind of pilgrimage
without sacred relics waiting at the end
– except for your own bones
and those of everyone you met along the way –
and that will have to do for you and me
as we move on, oddly separate, awkwardly one,
the timeless and the timed, into the mystery.

A Resurrection of a Kind

Say the worst
has already happened.
You are dead.
Zero is too big a number.

Now open your eyes –
shame you didn't realise
how good the day is
before you died.

Open the curtains
on a storm of light,
know the best was never
ahead or behind.

Now greet your beloved.
She's dead too
and her brief return
is the biggest lottery win ever.

You might as well
blow the lot today
because there is absolutely nothing
to save up for.

Her eyes, her smile,
her skin meeting yours –
how beautiful the dead are
while we live.

A Signing Off

That's me off, then.

You should not be surprised –
departure has long been
my nature and theme.

Surely you did not think
this could go on,
words condensing each morning,

breath on the chill panes
where you stood fingering your name,
or those evenings when

caresses like carrier pigeons
wheeled down the deepening
valley of your heart.

Those notes that passed
so freely between us,
gift them to charity, or oblivion.

Love and farewell –
next time we meet
I shall sing of arrival.